ROCKS, MINERALS, AND RESOURCES

Oil and Gas

John Paul Zronik

Crabtree Publishing Company
www.crabtreebooks.com

Crabtree Publishing Company
www.crabtreebooks.com

PMB 16A, 350 Fifth Avenue,
Suite 3308,
New York, NY 10118

612 Welland Avenue,
St. Catharines,
Ontario, Canada
L2M 5V6

73 Lime Walk,
Headington,
Oxford, 0X3 7AD
United Kingdom

Coordinating editor: Ellen Rodger

Editor: Carrie Gleason

Production coordinator: Rosie Gowsell

Designers: Brad Colotelo, Rosie Gowsell

Production assistant: Samara Parent

Proofreader and Indexer: Wendy Scavuzzo

Scanning technician: Arlene Arch-Wilson

Art director: Rob MacGregor

Photo research: Allison Napier

Prepress and printing: Worzalla Publishing Company

Consultants: Dr. Richard Cheel, Earth Sciences Department, Brock University

Project development: Focus Strategic Communications Inc

Contributors: Ron Edwards and Adrianna Edwards

Photographs: AP/Wide World Photos: p. 10 (top), p. 22 (right), p. 30 (middle); Bettmann/CORBIS/MAGMA: p. 9 (bottom), p. 10 (bottom); MARTIN BOND/SCIENCE PHOTO LIBRARY: p. 24 (top); Juan Castromil/Corbis/MAGMA: p. 29 (top); CORBIS/ MAGMA: p. 8; SIMON FRASER/SCIENCE PHOTO LIBRARY: p. 17 (bottom); Lowell Georgia/CORBIS/MAGMA: p. 16; Hulton Archive by Getty Images: p. 9 (right); Hulton-Deutsch Collection/ CORBIS/MAGMA: p. 14; Andy Johnstone: p. 20 (bottom); Wolfgang Kaehler:p. 23; Kit Kittle/CORBIS/MAGMA: p. 21; Scott F. Kohn: p. 15 (bottom); Larry Lee Photography/CORBIS/MAGMA: p. 19 (top); L. LEFKOWITZ/Getty Images: p. 27; J. Mead/Photo Researchers, Inc.: p. 31; Andrew McClenaghan/Photo Researchers, Inc.: p. 7; Jeroen Oerlemans: p. 28; Geoffrey Orth/Mira.com: p. 29 (bottom); Royalty-Free/Corbis: cover; Karen Robinson: p. 26; ROSHANAK.B/CORBIS SYGMA/ MAGMA: p. 18, p. 20 (top); Bill Ross/CORBIS/MAGMA: p. 12 (right); Royalty-Free/CORBIS/MAGMA: background image; CHRIS SATTLBERGER/SCIENCE PHOTO LIBRARY: p. 17 (top); Jacob Silberberg: p. 11 (bottom), title page; Jeff Smith/Getty Images: p. 15 (top); PETER STACKPOLE/TIME LIFE PICTURES: p. 12 (left); Superstock: p. 19 (bottom); Sven Torfinn: p. 11 (top), p. 29 (middle); Ami Vitale: p. 24 (bottom), p. 25 (bottom)

Illustrations: © Mark Crowshaw 2004 (represented by contactjupiter.com): p.22; Dan Pressman: p.6; Margaret Amy Reiach: p.3, pp.4-5;

Map: Jim Chernishenko: p.13

Cover: These workers on an oil rig are turning a crank that directs the drill.

Title page: Oil rig workers in China in the midst of a blowout.

Published by
Crabtree Publishing Company

Copyright © **2004**

Cataloging-in-Publication Data

Zronic. John Paul, 1972-
  Oil and gas / John Paul Zronic.
    p. cm. -- (Rocks, minerals, and resources)
  Includes index.
  ISBN 0-7787-1412-8 (rlb.) -- ISBN 0-7787-1444-6 (pbk.)
  1. Petroleum--Juvenile literature. I.Title. II. Series.
TN870.3.Z76 2004
553.2'82--dc22
                                2004000821
                                LC

Contents

The big blowout

As the drilling crew was eating dinner, they heard a hissing noise that soon grew into a shrill screech. They knew it was the sound of gas escaping from the oil well. Quickly leaving their meals, the crew members hurried to the scene. When they arrived, sticky black oil covered everything in sight. Oil was still spraying from the top of the well. It was a blowout.

Under pressure

Blowouts happen when oil wells, which are used to drill oil from the ground, are unstable, or when oil is first struck. About 70 years ago, blowouts, or gushers, were common. Blowouts happen when the **pressure** oil and gas are under below the ground is released, causing the oil and gas to shoot up to the surface. Today, modern technology allows people to **extract** oil and natural gas from the ground and transport them around the world. Oil is **refined** to produce gasoline that fuels cars and trucks. Natural gas provides heat **energy** for homes and factories. Oil and gas are the world's most important sources of energy. People go to great lengths to own and control their use.

5

What is oil?

Oil and natural gas are fossil fuels that are burned to provide energy. Natural gas is often found beneath the ground with oil. Oil is also called petroleum, or crude oil. Before oil and natural gas can be used as sources of energy, they are dug, or extracted, from the ground and processed into a useable form.

Fossil fuels began forming millions of years ago from the remains of plants and animals that once lived in the oceans. When the plants and animals died, they sank to the ocean floor, where over time they were covered by sediment, or **particles** of dirt and rock.

Oil and gas are trapped in layers of sedimentary rock under the ground.

natural gas

sedimentary rock

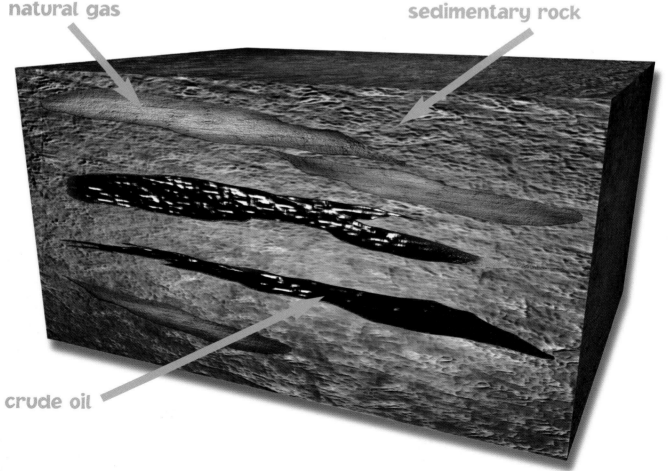

crude oil

Natural gas is a mixture of different gases. The most common gas is methane. Methane gas is sometimes called marsh gas because it is created from rotting marsh plants.

Layer upon layer

Eventually, many layers of sediment built up, increasing the pressure on the dead plants and animals. The combination of pressure and heat from deep inside the earth turned the once-living **organisms** into a thick brown waxy substance called kerogen. As the kerogen was heated to 212°Fahrenheit (100°Celsius), it separated into natural gas and a heavier liquid called crude oil.

Trapped!

Today, oil and natural gas are buried deep under the earth in areas where oceans existed millions of years ago. Oil and natural gas are trapped in layers of **sedimentary rock** called reservoirs. On top of the reservoir is a layer of non-**porous** rock, through which the oil and natural gas cannot pass. To get at the fossil fuels, people drill down through the rock to reach the reservoir.

Oil in history

People have been using oil for nearly 8,000 years. In ancient China, oil was burned for light and heat. About 3,000 years ago, people in China moved natural gas through bamboo pipes to burn for heating, lighting, and cooking.

Oil was used as a weapon of war by the ancient Persians and Greeks. The soldiers of these armies coated their arrows with oil and set them on fire. The flaming arrows were shot at enemies, killing people and destroying buildings and food stores.

The use of oil and gas as a fuel did not become big business until after 1859, when U.S. Colonel Edwin L. Drake drilled into the ground in Titusville, Pennsylvania, and struck oil. The first day of pumping at the site produced 25 barrels of oil. Soon after, a rush of oil **prospectors** descended on Pennsylvania. The area near where Drake made his find became known as Oil Creek. In 1862, the famous American businessman John D. Rockefeller started a company that refined the oil drilled from wells in Oil Creek.

Colonel Drake's drilled well resulted in a blowout. Blowouts like the one shown above are no longer common. In 1922, a BOP (Blowout Preventer) was invented in Texas. The BOP looked like a fire hydrant that screwed on top of the drilling well to stop the blowout.

Fuel for vehicles

One early use of oil was as a source of **kerosene**, which was burned for light. Oil soon became even more important, as it was used to make gasoline, a fuel for automobiles. Automobiles were first produced in 1908. Another product made from oil, called diesel fuel, became the main fuel for trains and ships. During the **World Wars**, demand for oil rose, as it was needed to power trains, trucks, aircraft, and military vehicles.

(right) Oil became an important fuel in the 1900s when cars, trucks, and buses became the main forms of ground transportation. This early Shell gas station is surrounded by oil derricks.

(left) The invention of the automobile accelerated the quest for oil. Like other vehicles, this Model-T car needed gasoline, refined from crude oil, to run.

9

Members of the Organization of Petroleum Exporting Countries (OPEC) meet to discuss prices and control of oil.

Demand for oil

As demand for oil grew during the 1900s, many countries began to use more than they produced. In the 1960s, a group of eleven oil-producing nations joined together to form an organization called OPEC (Organization of Petroleum Exporting Countries), which used its power to raise the price of oil. OPEC determines how much oil flows from wells in its member countries, and how much that oil will cost countries that need to buy it.

(right) Protesters from environmental organizations, such as Greenpeace, try to make people and oil companies aware of the dangers of possible oil leaks from drilling sites.

Oil companies

Oil companies and some countries go to great lengths to ensure control over the supply of oil. Oil is a resource that brings great wealth to a country. Oil was discovered in Saudi Arabia in 1933 by an American oil company. Saudi Arabia has one quarter of the world's known oil fields. All of the money from the sale of Saudi Arabia's oil is controlled by the country's royal family.

From the late 1940s until recently, the seven largest oil companies controlled the world's oil industry. They were called "the seven sisters": Mobil, Shell, British Petroleum, Exxon, Texaco, Chevron, and Gulf Oil. This Shell project is located in Nigeria.

The discovery of oil in West African countries such as Nigeria and Niger has done little to help most of the people of those countries. The refineries created jobs but they also brought pollution and caused fighting between people who do not benefit from oil money and those that do. In Nigeria, the government controls 60 percent of the country's oil. The rest is mostly controlled by large oil companies and a few small Nigerian oil companies.

Around the world

Crude oil and natural gas are found underground on land and below the ocean floor, or offshore. Since drilling for oil began in the 1850s, close to 50,000 oil fields have been discovered.

An oil field is a large or small reservoir of oil. Natural gas is most often found in the same area as oil, but in areas such as Eastern Europe, Canada, Australia, and Algeria, in Africa, natural gas exists in gas fields on its own.

This photograph of oil derricks was taken in California, U.S.A., in the 1930s.

Oil sands

Sometimes, oil is found on the Earth's surface, mixed with loose sand and a type of rock called sandstone. These oil deposits are called oil sands, or tar sands. Oil is difficult to separate from sand, which makes oil from oil sands expensive to process and purchase. The largest known oil sands are in western Canada.

These oil-drilling machines are called "nodding donkeys."

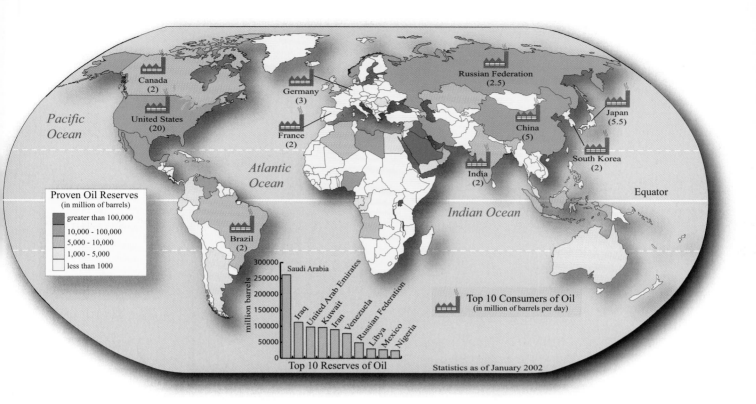

Proven Oil Reserves
(in million of barrels)

- greater than 100,000
- 10,000 - 100,000
- 5,000 - 10,000
- 1,000 - 5,000
- less than 1000

Top 10 Reserves of Oil

Top 10 Consumers of Oil
(in million of barrels per day)

Statistics as of January 2002

Where is the oil?

Most oil in the world exists in a few very large oil fields, many in Middle Eastern countries such as Saudi Arabia, Iraq, the United Arab Emirates, Kuwait, and Iran. Millions of years ago this oil began to form when the whole area of the Middle East was under the Tethys Sea, an ancient sea that no longer exists.

Beneath today's ocean floors, there are large oil fields in the Arabian Gulf, the Gulf of Mexico, and the North Sea.

Countries that produce, or extract, the most oil are Saudi Arabia, Russia, the United States, Iran, and China. Some countries without any oil **reserves**, such as France and Japan, must buy it from oil producing countries. Even the United States, which has oil, has been **importing** it from other countries since the 1970s, when it began using more oil than it could produce. The United States uses more oil and gas than any other country in the world.

(above) World map with countries that produce and use the most oil.

Exploration

Before the 1900s, people used simple tools such as shovels and picks to dig for oil near places were it had seeped to the Earth's surface. Seepages were the only way people knew oil existed in an area in the early days of exploration. Today, technology allows people to find oil that is buried deep underground.

A geologist, in this 1950s photo, places sensitive recording devices, called geophones, into the ground. Geophones gave information on how much oil is under the ground.

Oil geologists

Oil geologists are people who find oil by studying rock deep below the Earth's surface. To find oil, geologists must find sedimentary rock, which can contain oil. Oil geologists use a number of scientific tests and tools to see if the rock contains oil.

Measuring magnetic pull

Geologists use a magnetometer to measure changes in the Earth's **magnetic field**. Different types of rock have different effects on the magnetic field. Oil-containing sedimentary rock has a weak magnetic field.

Gravity meters

Oil geologists use a gravimeter to measure the pull of **gravity** on rock. Geologists can tell what type of rock lays below the surface of the Earth by measuring gravity around it. Non-porous rock increases the pull of gravity, while porous rock decreases gravity's pull. A low reading on the gravimeter could mean rocks in an area contain oil.

(right) Geologists collect on-site data.

(above) Geologists use computers to build maps of the Earth's layers.

Seismic surveys

Another way geologists determine the type of rock below the Earth's surface is by sending **shock waves**, called seismic waves, into the ground. The shock waves travel through the earth and reflect back to the surface at different rates depending on the type of rock they travel through. By measuring the speeds of the echo, geologists know what may lie under the surface. This is called a seismic survey.

There are three main ways to send shock waves into the ground: through vibroseis trucks, compressed air guns, and explosives. Vibroseis trucks have large metal plates under them which repeatedly hit the ground to create the vibrations.

(above) Vibroseis trucks send shock waves deep underground.

An exploratory well set up over the ocean to determine the location of oil.

Rocking the ocean floor

To send shock waves into the ocean floor, **compressed** air guns are used to shoot strong pulses of air into the water. On land and in the ocean, explosives are detonated to send out shock waves.

Over the ocean, geologists listen for the return echo of shock waves with sensitive microphones called hydrophones. On land, seismometers, which are instruments that record the shaking of the earth, are read by geologists for signs of oil and gas.

This geologist is trying to access an oil field in the frozen Arctic. Exploration in remote areas is very expensive as special equipment has to be brought there.

Exploratory wells

In areas where geologists have determined oil and natural gas are most likely to be, an exploratory well is drilled. This single well allows scientists to take rock samples and tell for certain if oil is buried there.

Drilling for oil

Drilling is the only way to tell for sure if for oil and gas are underground. There is only a one-in-ten chance that oil will be found in an area recommended for drilling by a geologist. Even if oil is found, there is only a one-in-50 chance there will be enough oil to make further drilling profitable.

The drilling site

After a drilling site on land is chosen, it is cleared and leveled using bulldozers. In many cases, roads are built to get people and equipment to and from the area. A drilling site also needs water and power sources, and depending on the location, living quarters for workers may need to be built.

The oil rig

The device used to extract oil from the Earth is called an oil rig. An oil rig is made up of many parts. The drill that burrows into the ground from an oil rig is made up of screwed together pieces of hollow steel pipe called a drill string. At the bottom of the drill string is a drill bit, usually made up of three cones of steel, each with sharp teeth that can cut through rock. The drill string is hung from a steel tower called a derrick. An engine provides power to rotate the drill string.

An oil field is a region that is rich in petroleum deposits.

18

The workers on this oil rig are positioning the drill.

Drilling down

As the drill string turns, the drill bit cuts away at underground rock. At the same time, mud is pumped down the drill string, forcing soil and rock to the surface. As the drill bit burrows deeper underground, more sections of hollow steel pipe are added to the drill string. A steel cable that extends from pulleys inside the derrick raises and lowers the drilling equipment.

Occasionally, blowouts still occur when drilling for oil, such as at this oil field in China.

Offshore drilling

There are four ways oil can be drilled beneath the ocean floor. It is very expensive to drill offshore.

Jack-up rigs are oil rigs that sit on a floating platform with steel legs that can be adjusted up or down. Jack-up rigs are towed by boat to the drilling site. Then, the rig's legs are lowered to rest on the ocean floor, raising the platform above the surface of the water, and providing a stable base for drilling.

Semi-submersible rigs are also used to drill for oil under the oceans. Semi-submersible rigs are mounted on **ballast tanks** to keep the rig afloat. Anchors help hold the rig in position.

(top) Offshore drilling rigs, such as this one in the Caspian Sea between Europe and Asia, take many months to assemble.

(right) Offshore drilling is dangerous when workers have to repair equipment at sea.

Drill ships

On a drill ship, the derrick and other drilling equipment is installed on the deck of a ship, and the drill string is lowered through an opening in the bottom of the ship. Onboard computers communicate with **satellites** to ensure a drill ship stays in its proper position.

A drill ship is a vessel that does not need to anchor itself to the seabed to drill for oil.

Production platforms

Once it is determined an area offshore contains enough oil to make drilling profitable, fixed production platforms are constructed. Barges take sections of the platform to the drilling site, where it is pieced together. Each production platform can drill more than 40 individual wells. Production platforms use a series of smaller tubes and pipes to force oil to the surface.

Refining oil

A refinery is where oil and gas are cleaned and separated into different fuels. Sometimes, refineries are located near an oil field. Most often, oil and gas are transported long distances to the refinery for processing.

The separation of oil into various fuels is done through a process called fractional distillation. This process happens in a distillation tower or column. Oil is heated until it boils at the bottom of the distillation tower. When the different substances that make up oil, called fractions, boil, they turn from a liquid state into a gas and rise up the tower.

Distillation Tower

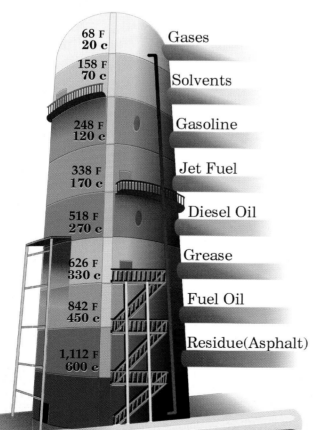

Temperature	Product
68 F / 20 c	Gases
158 F / 70 c	Solvents
248 F / 120 c	Gasoline
338 F / 170 c	Jet Fuel
518 F / 270 c	Diesel Oil
626 F / 330 c	Grease
842 F / 450 c	Fuel Oil
1,112 F / 600 c	Residue(Asphalt)

As the gas moves up the tower it cools, turning back into liquid form. The fractions return to a liquid at different temperatures, which keeps them separate from one another. Thicker fractions remain near the bottom of the distillation tower when they return to liquid form; lighter fractions, including **solvents** and gases, travel higher up the tower.

(above) A worker inspects the tanks and distillation towers at a refinery.

(left) Products are refined at different temperatures in a distillation tower.

Oil products

The fractional distillation of oil at a refinery produces a number of substances, each with its own use. Thick residue collected at the bottom of a distillation tower is turned into asphalt, used in constructing and repairing roads and highways. Grease, or lubricating oil, also separates from other fractions at the bottom of a distillation tower. Grease is used to lubricate machines with moving parts. Further up the distillation tower, diesel oil separates from other fractions. Diesel oil is used as fuel for trucks and buses, and also as heating fuel.

Oil refineries are busy places, even at night. The lights on this refinery show the towers, pipes, and storage tanks of the plant.

Gasoline is a fraction of crude oil that separates near the top of the distillation tower. Gasoline is the most valuable because people around the world depend on a steady supply for their vehicles. After gasoline is separated from oil, chemicals such as sulphur and lead are removed before it can be used as fuel for vehicles.

At this hospital in Azerbaijan, a country in eastern Europe, patients are treated to oil baths which they believe cure illnesses.

Solvents

The two lightest fractions of oil, or those which travel to the highest level in the distillation tower are solvents and gases. These gases are called substitute natural gas, which means they can be made from other fossil fuels, such as oil and coal, but are not found in a gaseous state in nature as natural gas is.

Making plastics

Solvents can be treated and turned into chemicals, and are also used to make nylon and plastics. Gases are the lightest of all the fractions that make up oil, and are compressed and bottled after separation.

Gases are used for heating, cooking, and even as fuel in lighters. Gases separated in the distillation tower are also treated and used to make some kinds of plastics.

Refining natural gas

Natural gas is cleaned of impurities and water. When natural gas is extracted from the ground, it is clear and odorless. A chemical is added to natural gas to give it a foul smell. Gas is flammable, which means it catches fire and burns easily.

At this factory in oil-rich Azerjaijan, plastic sheeting is made from petroleum.

Pipelines and tankers

Over land, oil and natural gas are moved through pipelines from wells to refineries. To cross water, oil is moved in large tanker ships. Natural gas is cooled into a liquid form at the oil or gas well and shipped in refrigerated tankers over water.

Pipelines

Oil is transported over land through surface and underground pipelines. A pipeline is the easiest way to move crude oil over land. The United States has about 219,000 miles (352,446 kilometers) of pipeline that transports oil. The pipe that makes up a pipeline measures about three feet (one meter) across. Using a system of pumps and valves, oil is transported through a pipeline at a speed of five miles per hour (eight kilometers per hour).

Pumping stations are located at regular intervals along the pipeline. Pipelines in cold parts of the world are insulated to keep oil from becoming too cold and thick to move through them.

The Trans-Alaska Pipeline moves oil 800 miles (1,290 km) from northern Alaska to Port Valdez. The pipeline keeps the oil moving despite the extreme cold temperature of the north.

Natural gas

A high-pressure pipeline is the easiest way to transport natural gas from the place it is discovered to people who use it. Natural gas pipelines consist of sections of steel pipe welded together and laid in trenches. Compressors are sometimes used to help push natural gas through a pipeline. Pipelines can also transport natural gas through bodies of water. Offshore natural gas pipelines are built in trenches on the seabed using a floating vessel called a laybarge.

Natural gas is piped to cities and towns through a large pipe called a gas main. The gas is stored in tanks until it is needed in homes and factories. Gas pipes under cities are made of strong plastic. Gas company employees monitor the pipes to make sure there are no leaks.

Tanker ships

Over water, oil is moved using giant tanker ships, called supertankers. Supertankers are built specifically to transport crude oil. One type of supertanker called a Very Large Crude Carrier, or VLCC, can hold more than 200,000 tons (181,437 tonnes) of oil. Even larger supertankers called Ultra Large Crude Carriers, or ULCC, can transport more than 300, 000 tons (272,155 tonnes).

(above) Oil is transported by pipeline to ports. From there, it is shipped by barge all over the world.

Pollution

When oil is burned to provide energy in power plants or to fuel vehicles, it creates gases harmful to the environment, such as sulphur dioxide, nitrogen oxides, carbon dioxide, and carbon monoxide. These substances cause health problems in plant and animal life, including people.

Acid rain

When fuel is burned in cars, exhaust, or waste gases, are dispersed into the air. Nitrogen oxide in the exhaust gases mixes with moisture in the air which rises up to form clouds. When the clouds release rain, the water is acidic, or poisonous. Acid rain pollutes lakes and kills fish living in the water.

The greenhouse effect

Our planet is like a huge greenhouse. Heat from the sun is trapped by a gas called carbon dioxide in the **atmosphere**, keeping Earth warm. Carbon dioxide is also produced when fossil fuels are burned, which adds too much of the gas to the atmosphere. As a result, heat from the sun is trapped by the carbon dioxide overheating the planet. This overheating may cause the polar ice caps to melt, which will flood ocean shorelines, possibly even swamping major coastal cities.

The burning of fossil fuel is a major cause of pollution.

Oil spills

Oil can harm the environment in other ways, such as when oil spills from a tanker or pipeline into the ocean. Oil spills kill ocean life, coating birds and polluting the water sea animals swim in. Oil and water do not mix, so oil spilled into the ocean floats on top of the water. Many spills are contained by surrounding the oil with a floating barrier called a boom, which keeps oil from spreading outward. Detergents can be used to disperse spilled oil. If oil spilled from a tanker or pipeline reaches shore, it is scraped from beaches and blasted off rocks using water. Over time, tiny animals living in the ocean break the oil down.

Oil spills have a disastrous effect on animal life (above) and plants (below).

Cleaning up after an oil spill is a long and difficult process.

29

Alternatives to oil

Scientists estimate that the world will use up its supply of oil and natural gas in less than 100 years. Earth does not make oil as fast as humans use it, so people are being forced to look to alternative sources of energy.

Transportation

The biggest use of oil is as fuel for automobiles. Before the world runs out of oil, people will have to find other ways of powering their vehicles. Some cars that have recently been developed, called hybrids, use only a fraction of the gasoline that other cars use, relying mostly on battery power. Other cars that use no fossil fuels at all are powered by fuel cells. Fuel cells create electricity by combining **hydrogen** and oxygen.

Hybrid cars use a combination of electrical batteries and gasoline engines to help reduce harmful fuel emissions. Cars that are not fuel efficient use too much oil and pollute the environment.

Nature's energy

Solar, or sun power, and wind power are two sources of energy that are free and will never run out. Solar power can be harnessed through solar panels, which collect and store the sun's energy.

Large turbines turned by the power of the wind create energy that is used to make electricity. The problem with these two sources of energy is that they require large tracts of land and specific weather conditions to work.

Biogas

Natural gas is mostly made up of methane gas.

Methane gas results when plants decay in places where there is not very much oxygen, such as marshes and deep under the seabed. People can create methane gas in a vessel called a biogas generator, or digester, where animal waste and plants are placed, warmed, and deprived of oxygen until a gas is created. The gas can then be used as fuel.

What is renewable?

Natural resources are materials supplied by nature. Examples of natural resources are water, trees, and fossil fuels. Some natural resources will replenish themselves when used carefully by people, such as forests, which will grow back after they have been cut down and the trees used for timber. Fossil fuels are non-renewable resources. This means that once they are used up, they are gone forever.

Solar panels are specially designed glass panes that use the sun's energy to create electricity for homes and businesses. Solar energy is a renewable energy source that does not harm the environment.

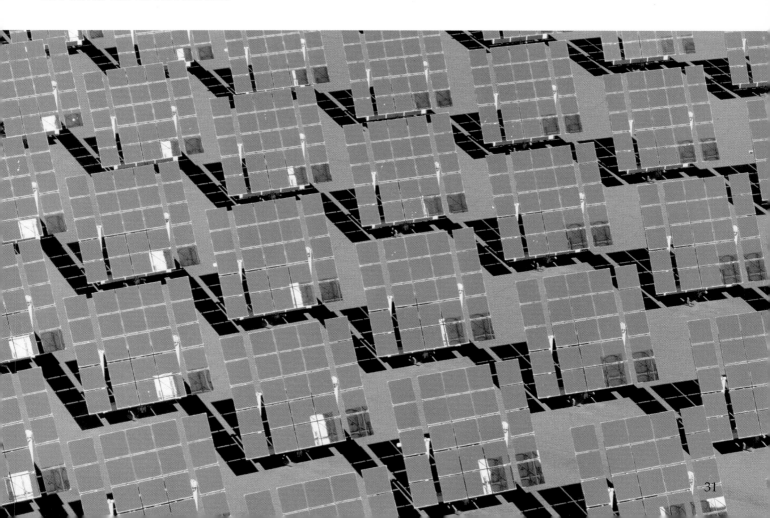

Glossary

atmosphere The layer of gases that surround Earth

balast tanks Tanks on ships that fill or empty with water to raise or lower the vessel

compress To squeeze tightly together

energy Usable power

environment The air and living things around us

extract To pull out or separate

fossil fuels Natural fuels formed millions of years ago from the remains of living things

gravity The invisible force that pulls all things toward Earth

hydrogen A very light colorless, odorless gas

import To bring into a country from another country

kerosene A flammable oil used as fuel

magnetic field The area around a magnetic body in which the pull of the magnet can be felt

organism A living being

particle The smallest bit of something

porous Full of holes

pressure Weight pushing down on an object

process To treat or make by a special series of actions

profitable Able to make money

prospectors People who explore areas looking for something valuable, such as oil or valuable minerals

refine To free from impurities or unwanted material

reserves Things set aside for a later date

sedimentary rock A type of rock formed from the build up and eventual compression of many layers of sediment

satellite An object launched into space that orbits Earth and sends back data

seep To pass slowly through tiny openings

shock waves Powerful waves of energy

solvent A substance that dissolves or disperses another substance

World Wars A set of international conflicts from 1914-1918 and from 1939-1945 in which many people were killed

Index

1 2 3 4 5 6 7 8 9 0 Printed in the USA 0 9 8 7 6 5 4 3 2 1